ISBN 0-86163-631-7 (cased)

This edition first published 1993 by
Award Publications Limited,
The Old Riding School, Welbeck Estate,
Nr Worksop, Nottinghamshire

First published 1990 by Hodder and Stoughton
Children's Books

Printed in Singapore

FRUIT

Christine Butterworth

Illustrated by Barbara Walker

AWARD PUBLICATIONS LIMITED

There are lots of different kinds of fruit. Some fruit is smooth and some is prickly. Some fruit is big, and some is small.

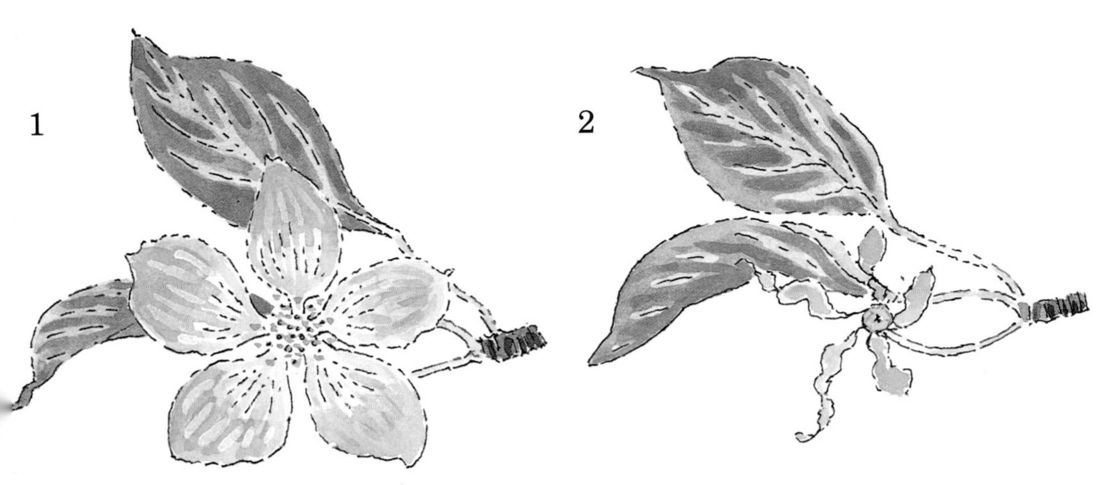

A fruit grows on a plant, after the flower has died. The middle of the dead flower turns into a seed. A soft, fleshy fruit grows around the seed to protect it.

A fruit can have lots of tiny seeds in it. Here are some fruits which have small seeds. You can eat both the fruits and the seeds.

These fruits have only one seed inside a hard stone.

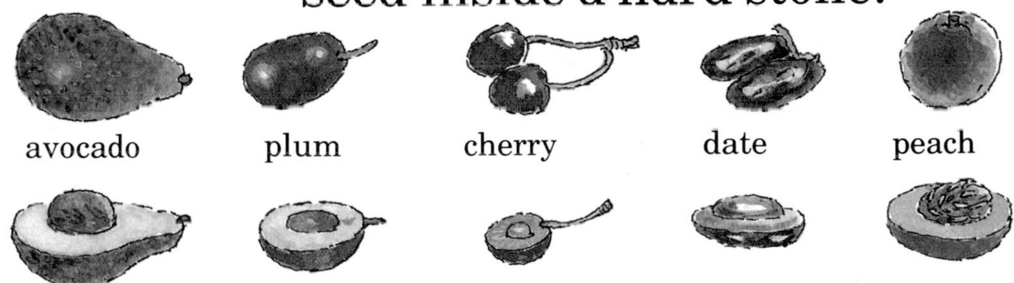

You cannot eat the stone, but if you crack it you will find the seed.

Some fruit has a thick skin you must peel off before you eat it.

Some fruit has a thin skin. You can pop it straight into your mouth. (It is best to wash it first.)

Daisy and her mum want to buy some fruit to make a fruit salad. This supermarket sells fruit which has been grown all over the world.

Pomegranates grow on trees,
in hot places such as Israel
and Cyprus.

Inside the pomegranate, there is a soft pink juicy jelly packed with seeds. You can eat the seeds and the jelly.

Daisy chooses a kiwi fruit. It has a thin, hairy skin and bright green flesh which tastes sharp and sweet. You can eat the tiny black seeds.

Kiwi fruit first grew on vines in China. Some people still call them Chinese gooseberries. Now a lot of kiwi fruit comes from New Zealand.

This part of the supermarket sells tropical fruit. It comes from parts of the world which are hot and sunny all year round.

Bananas are a tropical fruit grown mainly in Africa and Central America. They grow on tall trees in big bunches. One bunch may have over a hundred bananas!

Pineapples are tropical fruits, too. A pineapple grows on a plant with hard, spiky leaves. The pineapple grows on the end of a stiff stalk.

When fruit is squeezed, all the juice runs out. Do you like pineapple juice? Or is there another juice you prefer?

‘I need some dried fruit to make a cake,’ says Daisy’s mum. Sultanas, currants and raisins are all made from dried grapes.

The grapes are picked and laid out to dry in the hot sun. Dried fruit will keep for a long time. Which dried fruits have you eaten?

At home, Daisy helps to cut up the fruit for the fruit salad. Look at all the colours! Which fruits are in the bowl?

Fruit is good for you. It has lots of vitamins which help to keep you healthy. It also tastes nice.

'Let's try to grow something from our left-overs,' says Daisy. She cuts the top off the pineapple and stands it in a plate. The plate contains a little water to help it grow.

Daisy has some seeds too,
which she plants just under
the earth in pots.
'If we're lucky, some leaves
will grow.'

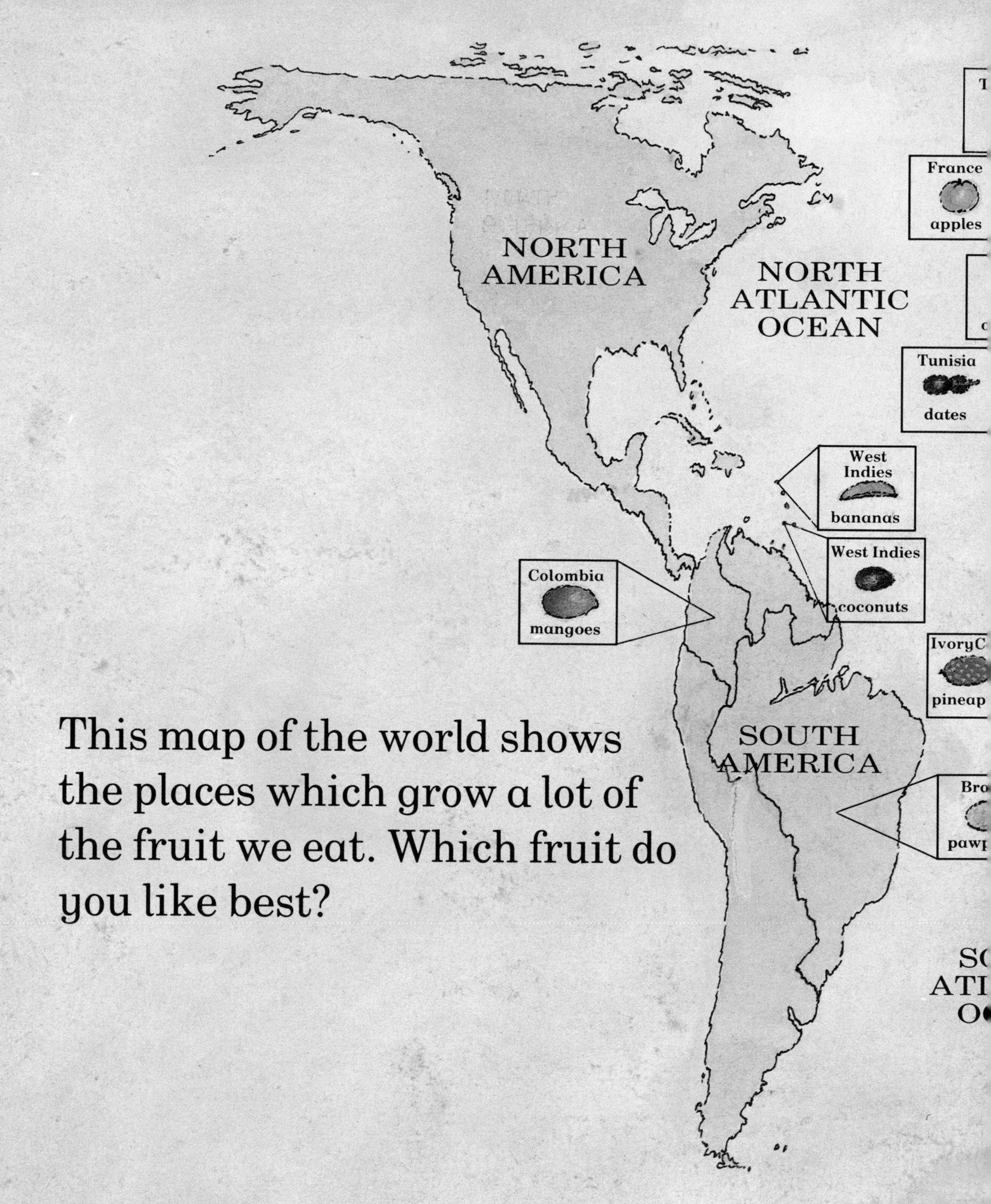

This map of the world shows the places which grow a lot of the fruit we eat. Which fruit do you like best?

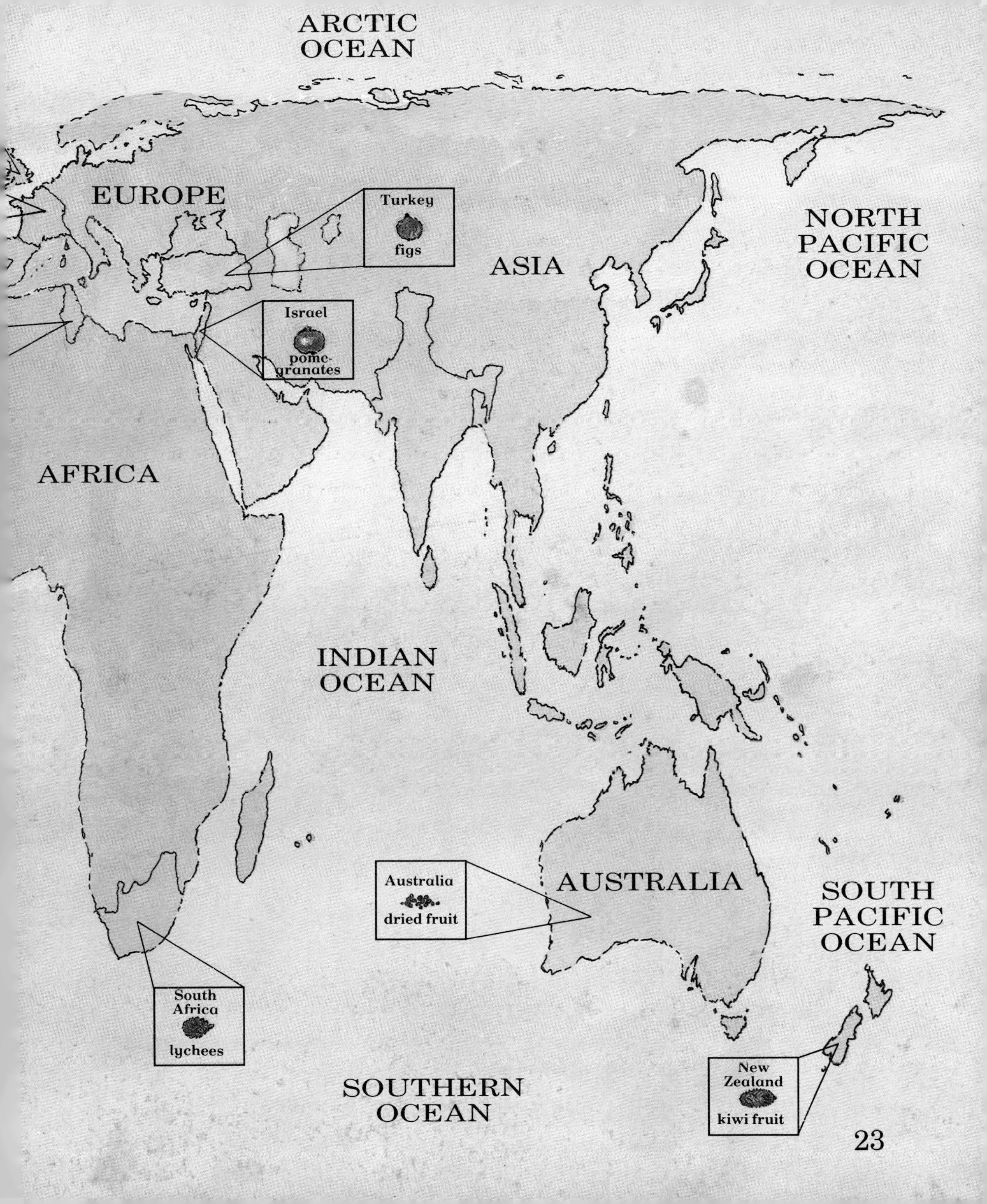
ARCTIC OCEAN
EUROPE
Turkey
figs
ASIA
NORTH PACIFIC OCEAN
Israel
pome-granates
AFRICA
INDIAN OCEAN
Australia
dried fruit
AUSTRALIA
SOUTH PACIFIC OCEAN
South Africa
lychees
New Zealand
kiwi fruit
SOUTHERN OCEAN

fruit words

dried fruit

fruit salad

pips

seeds

skin

stones

tropical fruit